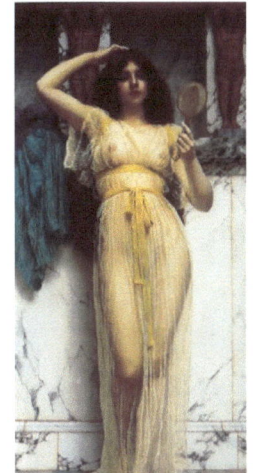

John William Godward

Edited by Lacey Belinda Smith

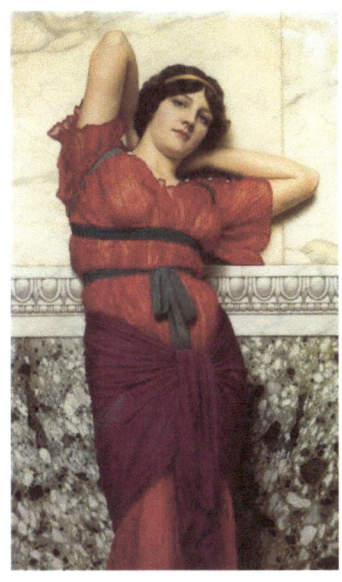
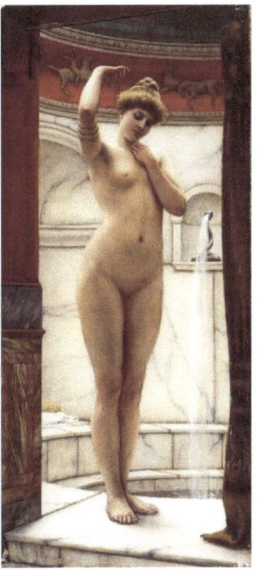

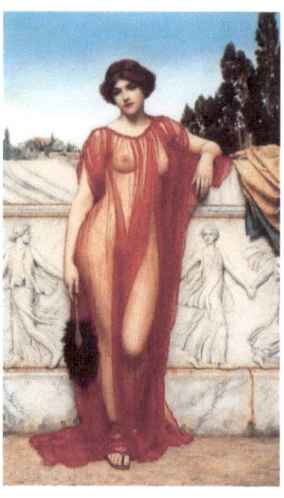

John William Godward (1861 –1922) was an English painter from the end of the Neo-Classical era. This artist was born of a wealthy family that expostulated his vocation of art. He was a member of the so-styled "Marble School," followers of Lawrence Alma-Tadema. This work concentrated almost exclusively on Classical Grecian or Roman subjects. Godward is best known for his highly finished paintings of pulchritudinous girls attired in classical robes. .He well accentuated the sensuality of the female form. He began exhibiting at the Royal Academy in 1887, and his work was greatly admired. By the beginning of the 20th century, Neo-Classicism was beginning to lose favour; and the modernist movement was taking over the art world. Godward moved to Rome in 1912, but he returned to England in 1919. He started to be tepidly received by critics, sales of his work slowed, and his health declined. He committed suicide in his studio by gassing himself at the age of 61.

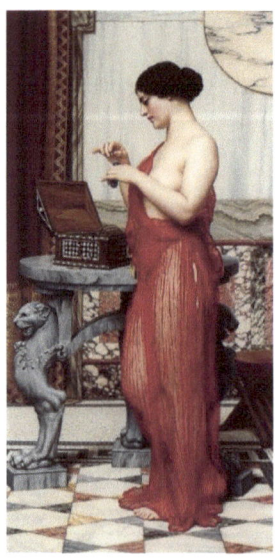

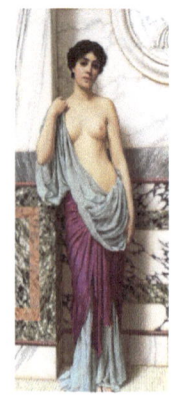

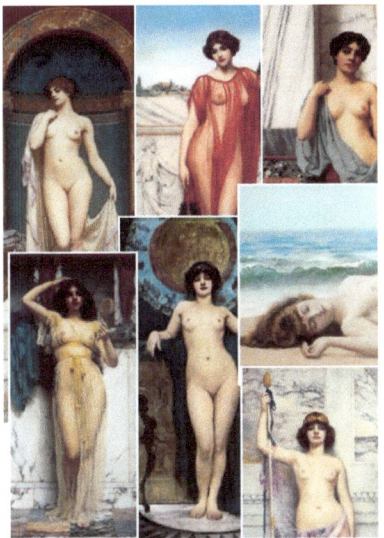

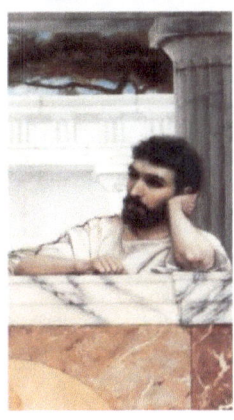

Waiting for an Answer, detail (putative self-portrait) - John William Godward

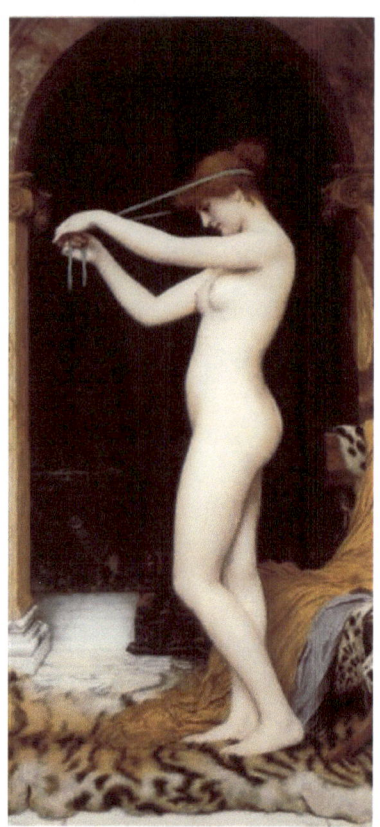

Venus Binding Her Hair—1897

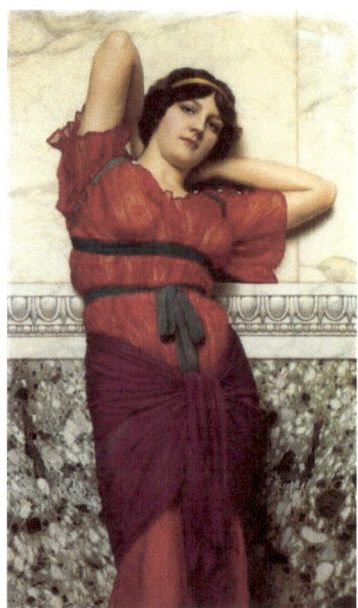

Contemplation—1922

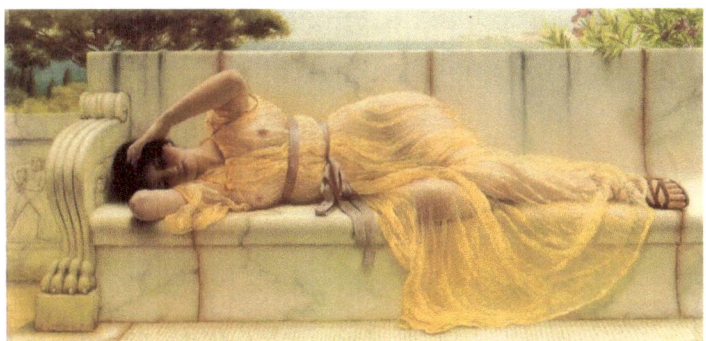

Girl In Yellow Drapery--1901

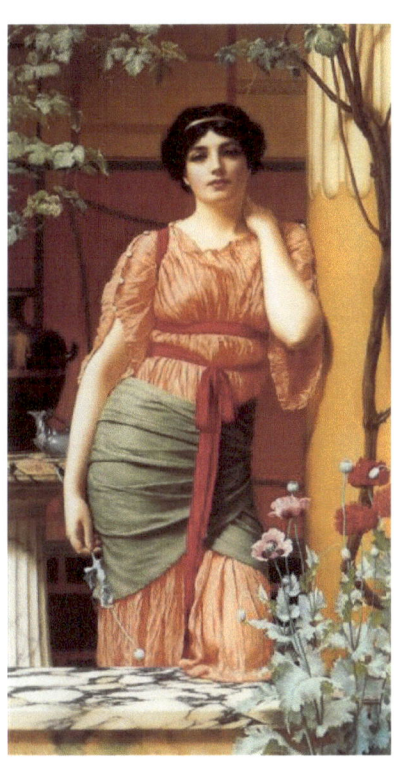

Nerissa—1906

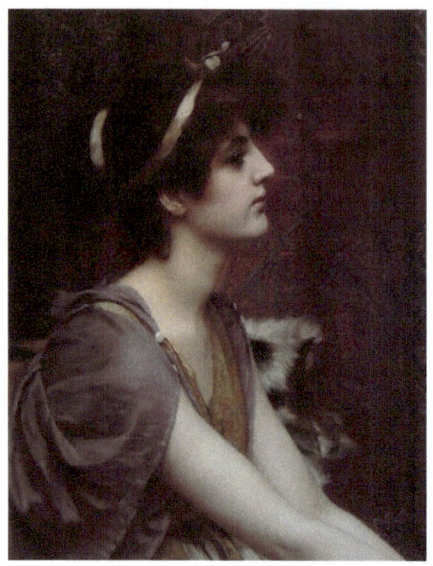

A Classic Beauty--1892

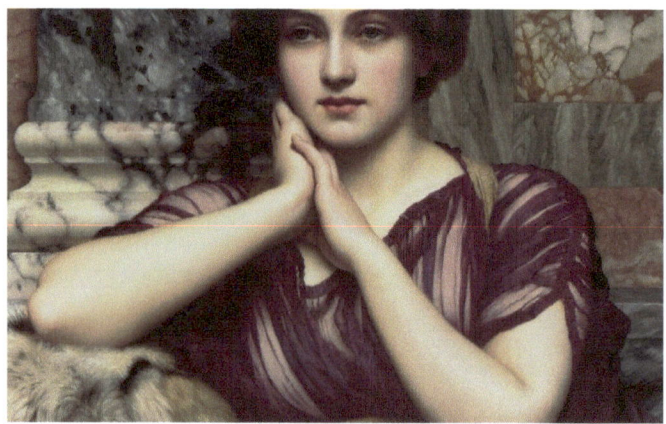

A Classic Beauty--1909

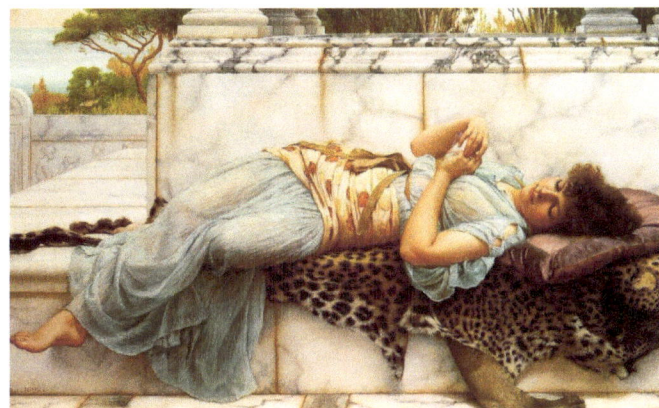

The Betrothed--1892

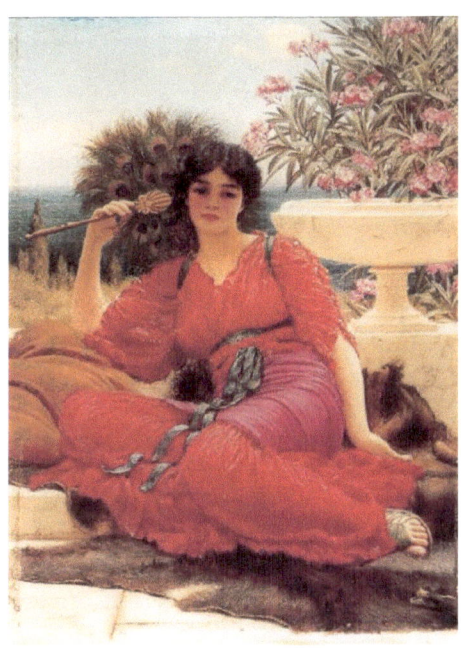

Flabellifer--1905

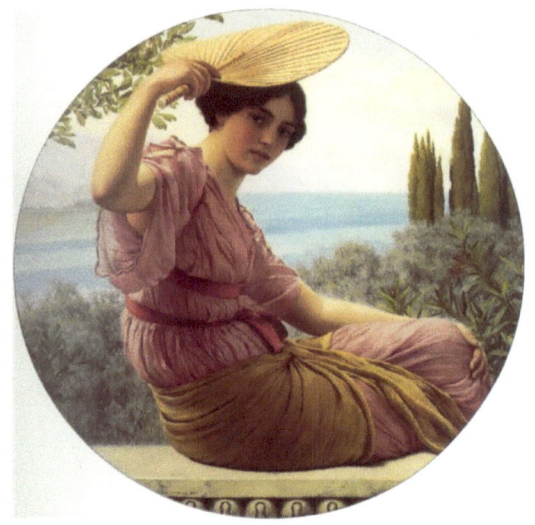

The Golden Hours—1913

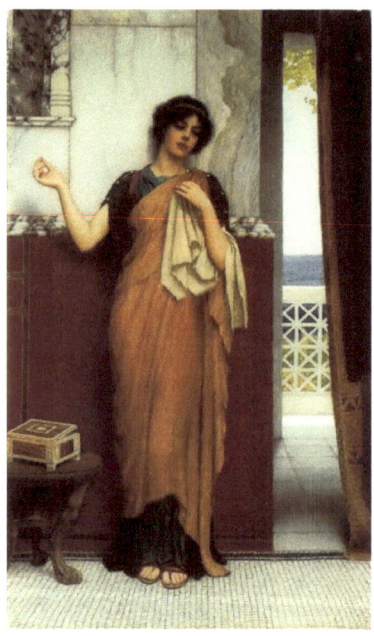

A Stitch In Time (Idle Thoughts)--1898

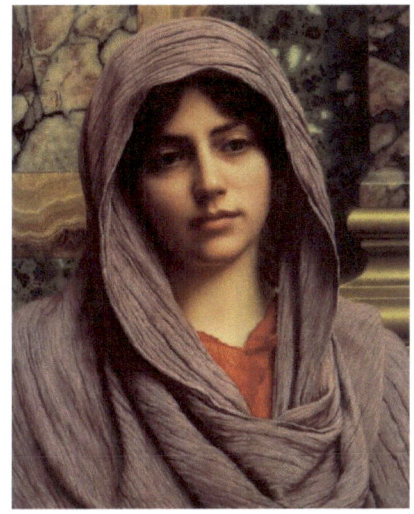

Lycinna—1918

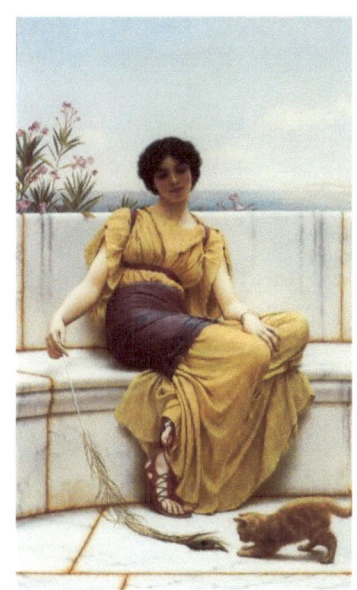

Idleness--1900

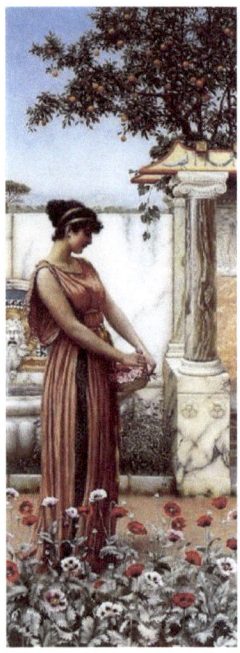

An Idle Hour—1890

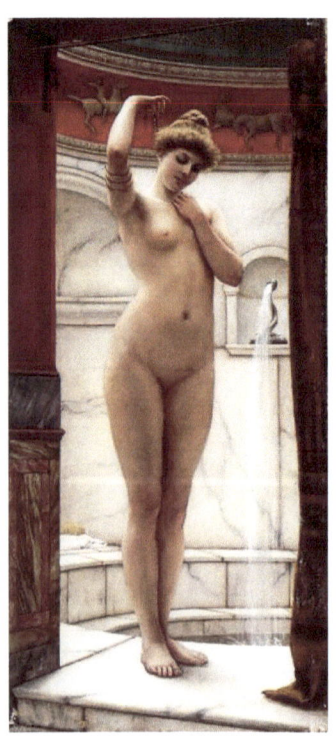

A Pompeian Bath--1890

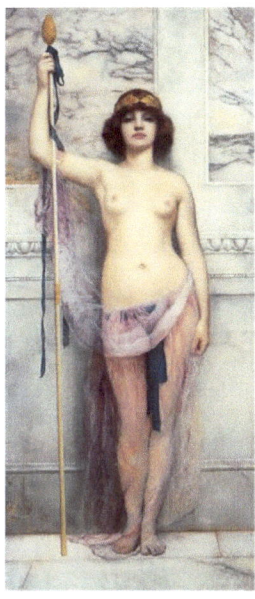

A Priestess—1893

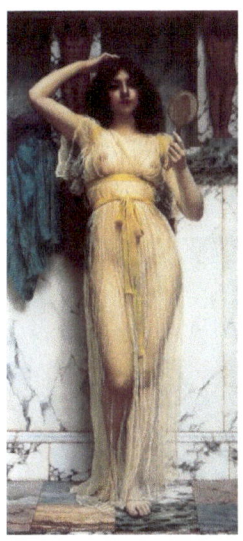

Girl With A Mirror--1892

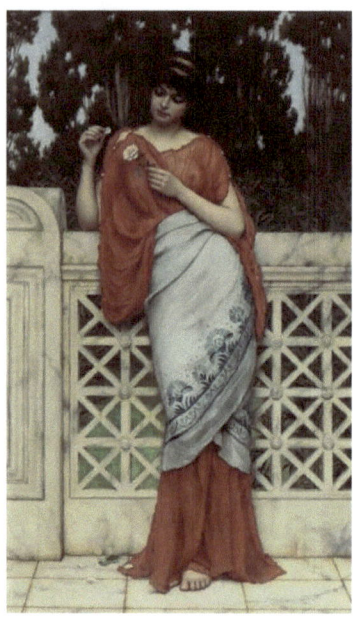

He Loves Me, He Loves Me Not—1896

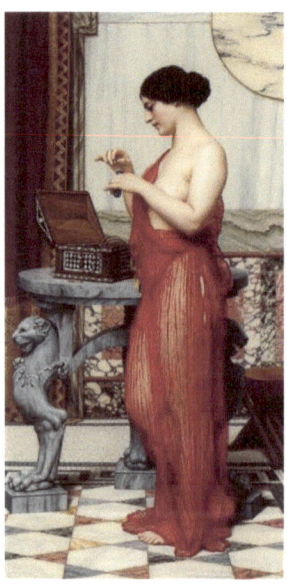

The New Perfume--1914

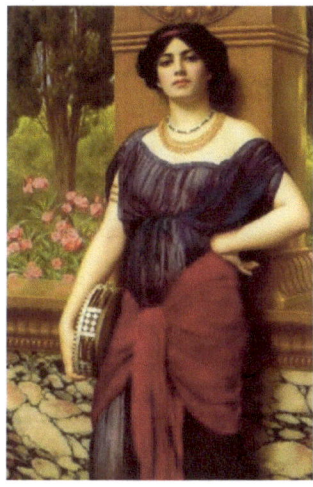

The Tambourine Player--1909

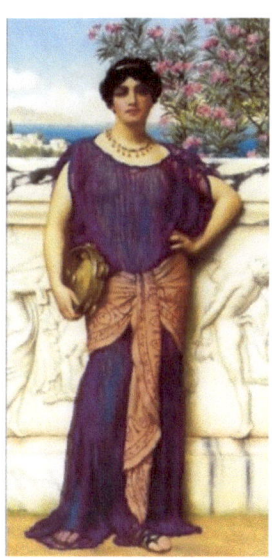

The Tambourine Girl—1909

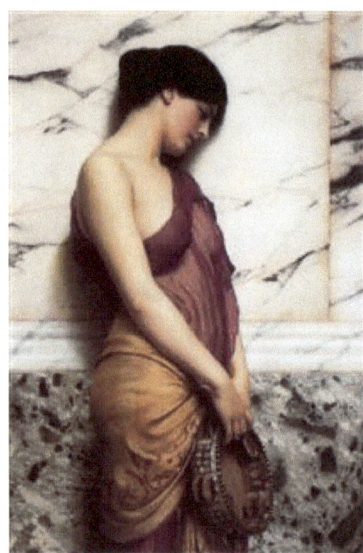

The Tambourine Girl--1906

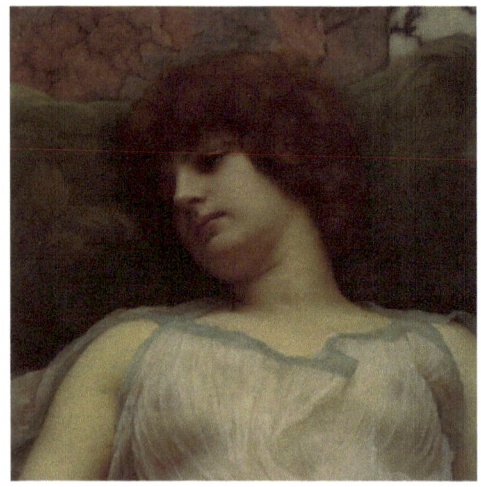

Idle Moments—1895

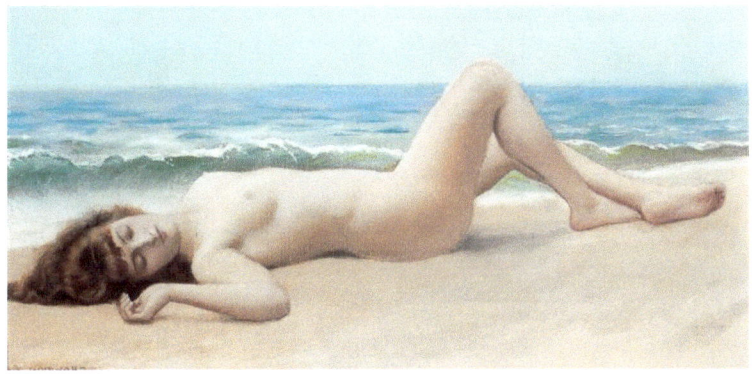

Nude On The Beach-- Nu Sur La Plage—1922

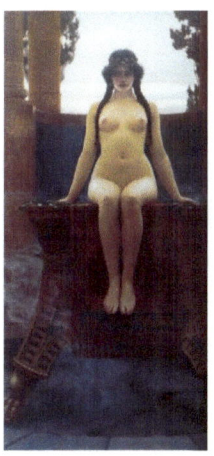

The Delphic Oracle—1899

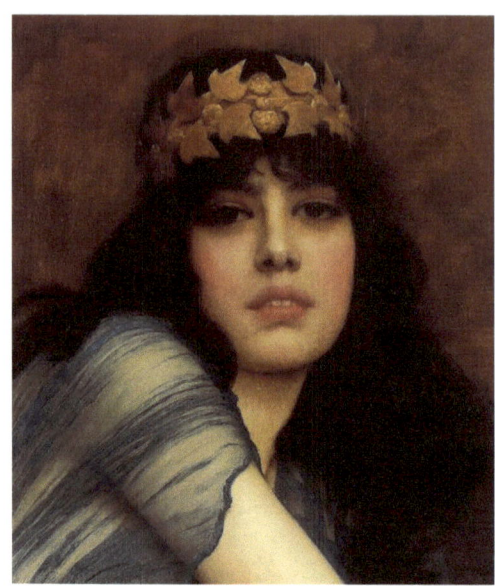

Head Of A Girl (Also Known As The Priestess)—1896

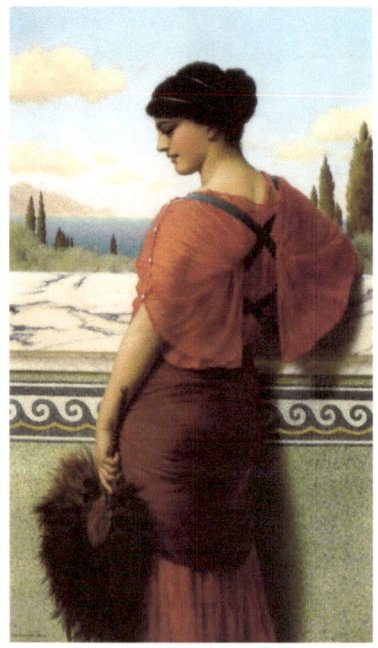

Phyleis--1908

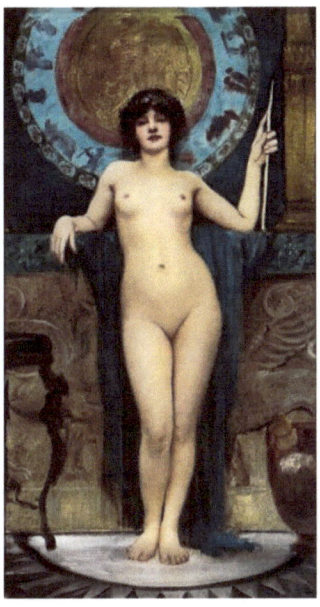

Study Of Campaspe

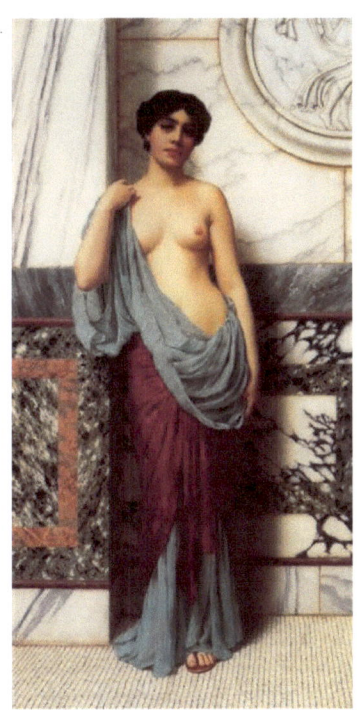

At The Thermae--1909

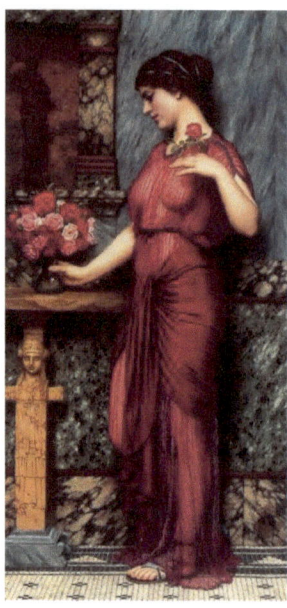

An Offering To Venus—1912

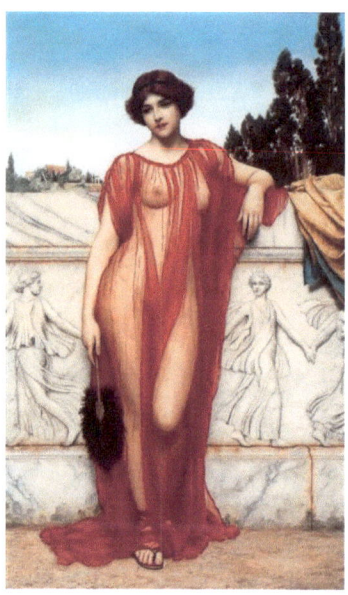

Athenais--1908

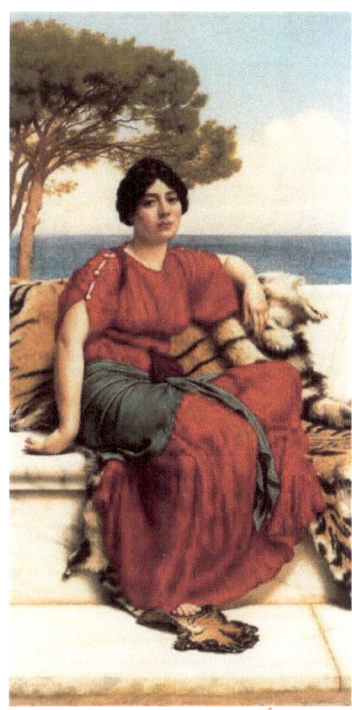

By The Blue Ionian Sea—1916

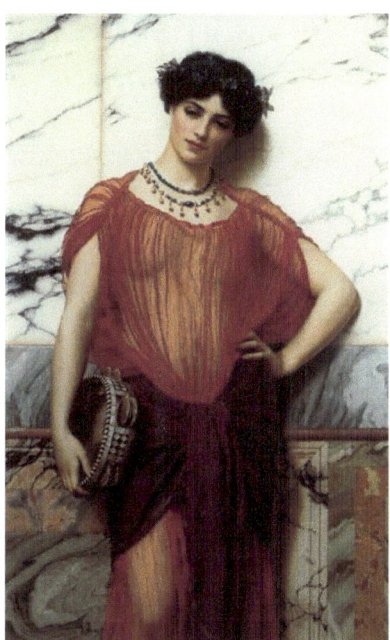

Drusilla--1906

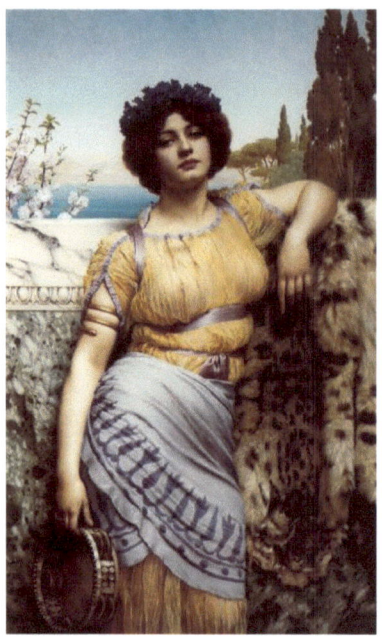

Ionian Dancing Girl--1902

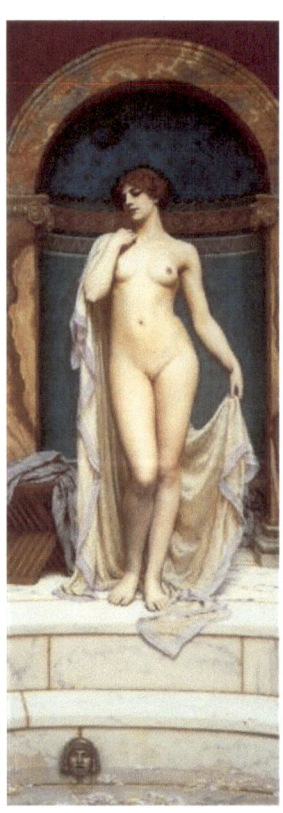

Venus At The Bath—1901

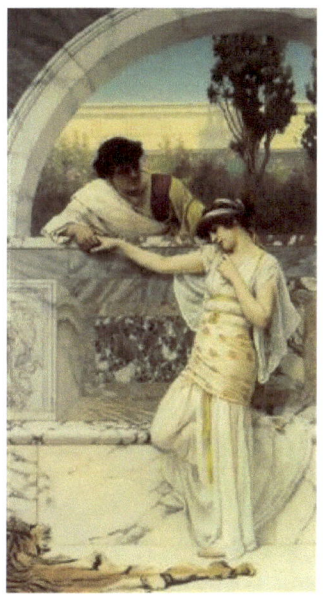

Yes Or No—1893

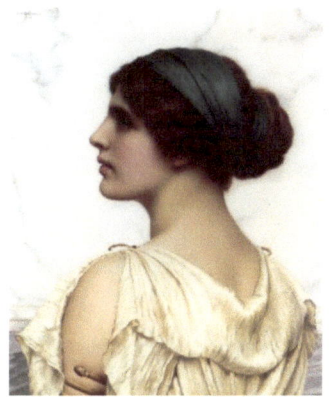

Atalanta--1908

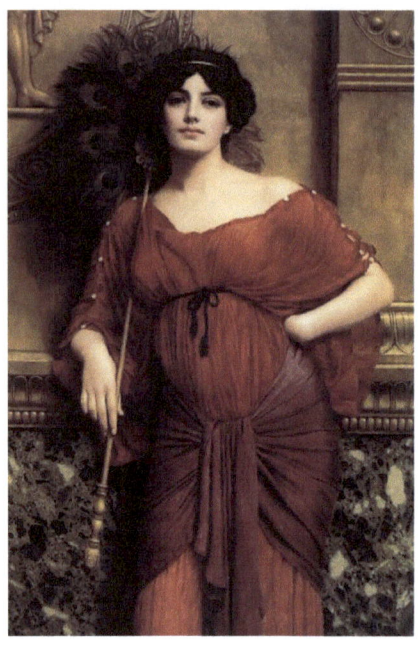

A Roman Matron—1905

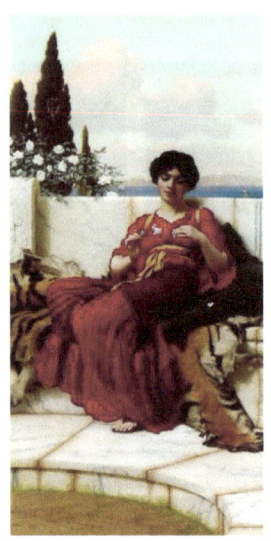

Mischief

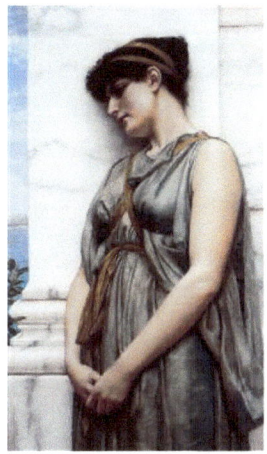

Pompeian Girl—1889

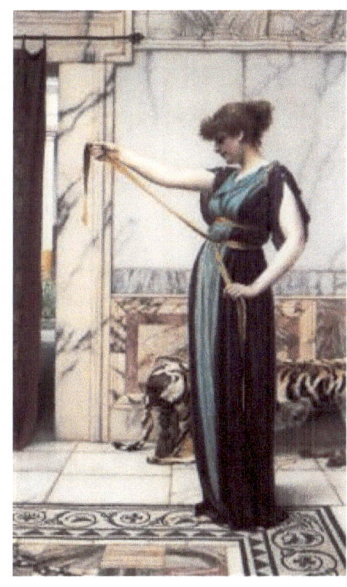

A Pompeian Lady—1891

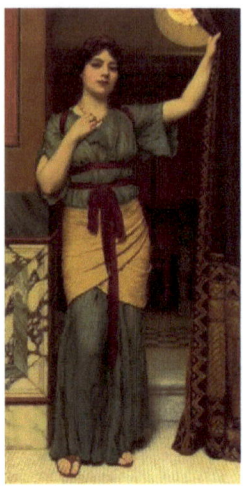

A Pompeian Lady --1916

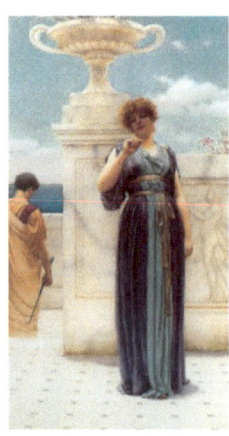

The Engagement Ring—1891

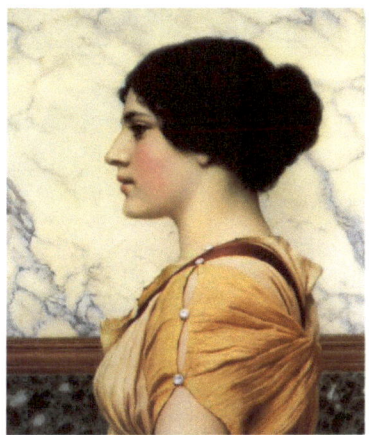

Cassotis

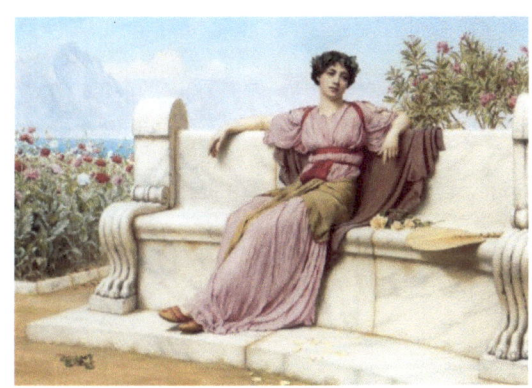

Tranquillity—1914

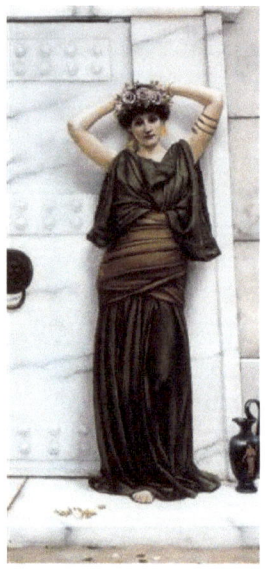

Ianthe—1889

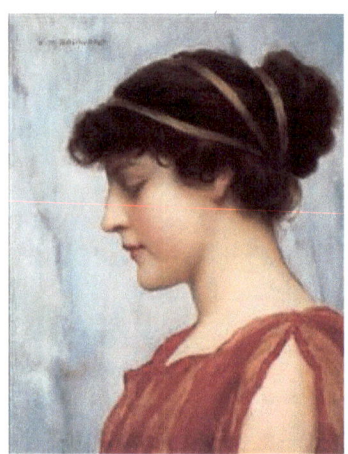

Ophelia—1889

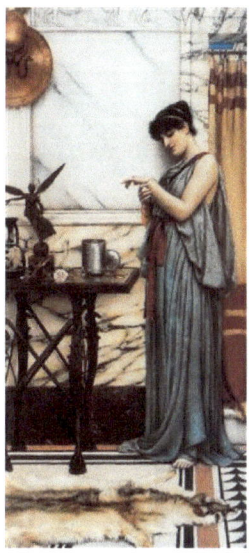

His Birthday Gift—1889

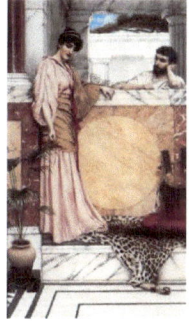

Waiting for an Answer—1889

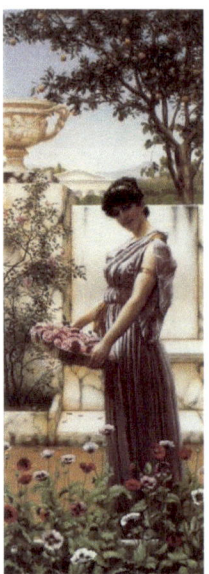

The Flowers of Venus--1890

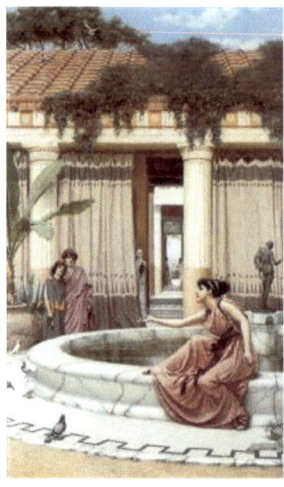

Innocent Amusements--1891

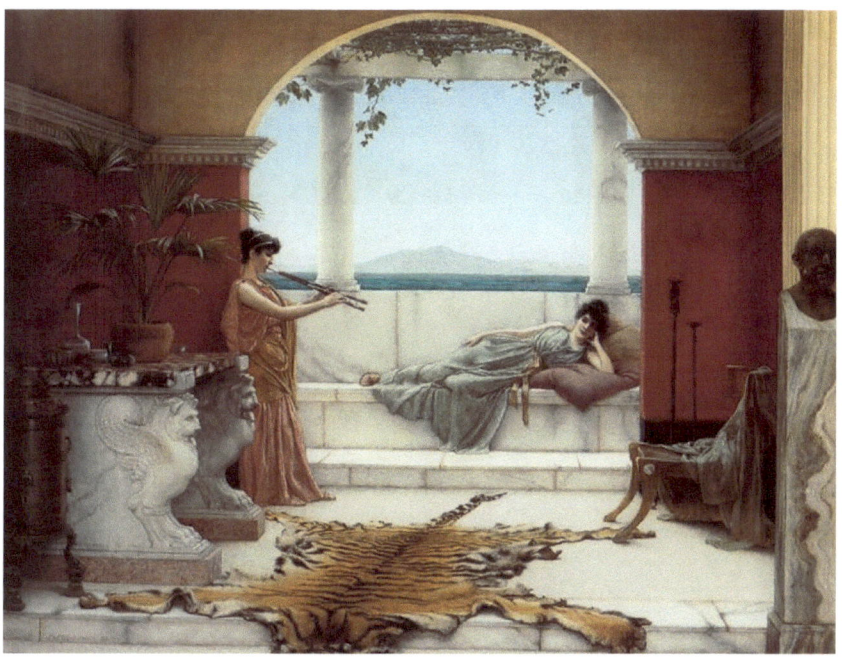

The Sweet Siesta of a Summer Day—1891

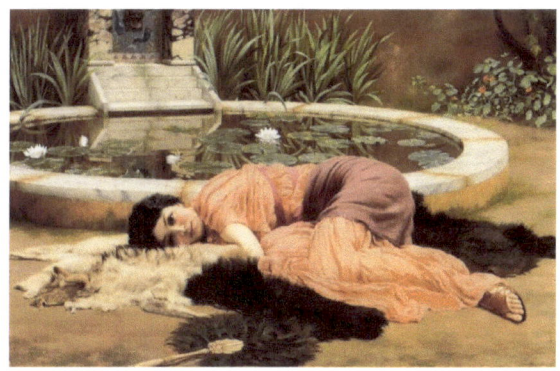

Dolce Far Niente—1904

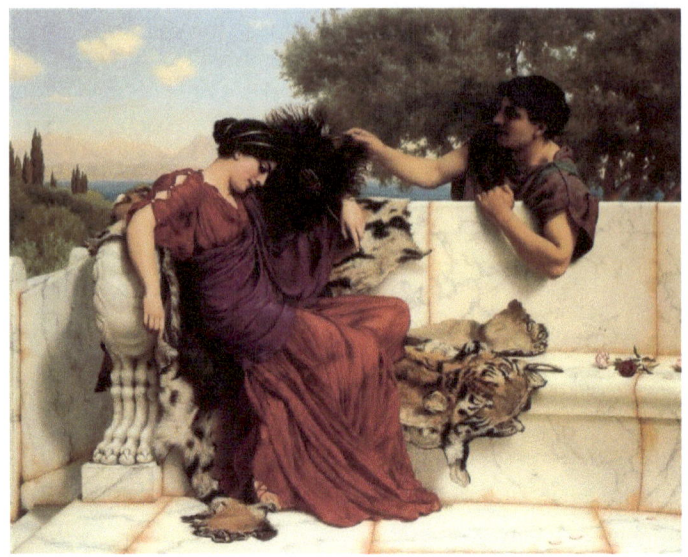

The Old, Old Story--1903

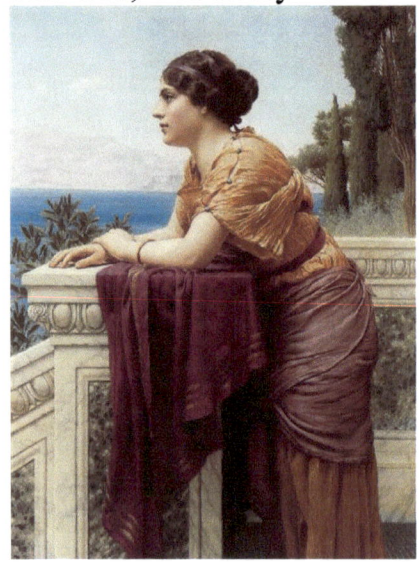

The Belvedere—1913

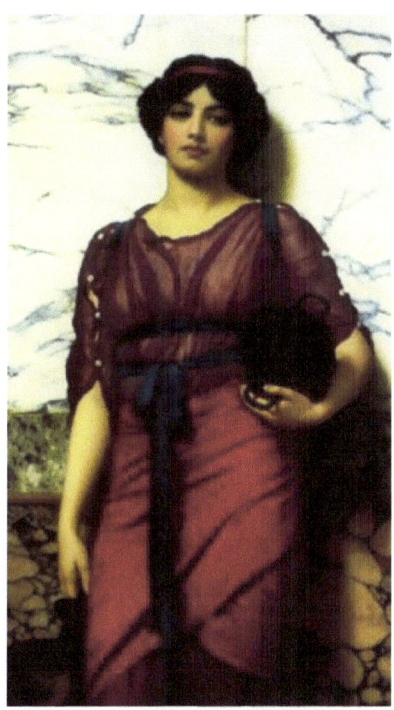

Grecian Idyll—1907

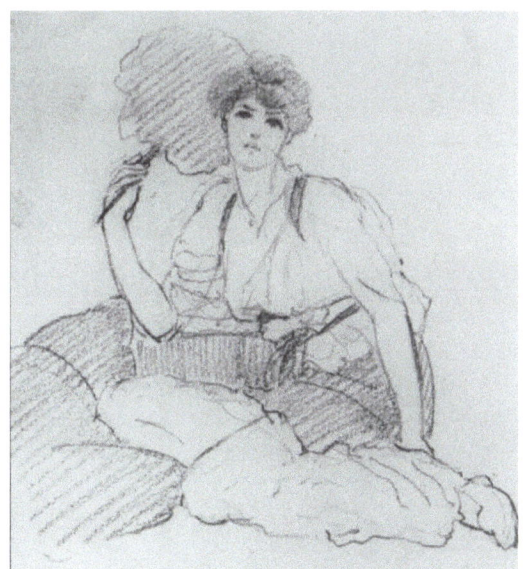

Flabellifera--1905